PEOPLE AT WORK

IN A
DEPARTMENT
STORE

DEBORAH FOX

EVANS BROTHERS LIMITED

Published by Evans Brothers Limited
2a Portman Mansions
Chiltern Street
London
W1M 1LE

First published in 2000

Commissioned by: Su Swallow
Design: Neil Sayer
Photography: Gareth Boden, Robert Wright
Illustrator: Liam Bonney/The Art Market

British Library Cataloguing in Publication Data

Fox, Deborah
  People at work in a department store
  1.Department stores - Juvenile literature 2.Department
  stores - Employees - Juvenile literature
  I.Title II.In a department store
  381.1'41

ISBN 0237519658

Printed in Hong Kong by Wing King Tong

Acknowledgements

The author and publisher wish to thank the following for their help:
Roger Simmonds, Robert Wright, Clare Campbell, Ruth Weatherley and all the staff at Heelas, Reading, a branch of the John Lewis Partnership.

All photographs by Gareth Boden except for the following:
page 8 bottom and page 9 left (Robert Wright); page 22 left (Heelas), page 27 top and bottom (Robert Wright).

Contents

The shop opens

I'm Ruth and I work in a large department store. I'm an assistant to the managing director and my job is to make sure all the 21 selling departments at this store display their stock clearly and effectively. If the stock is well presented, our sales are higher.

Stocking shelves

We sell a huge number of items every day and our shelves need to be re-filled. Some departments, like stationery, sell a lot of stock every day, but others, like lighting, sell fewer individual items. At 8 o'clock in the morning our vans bring over stock from the warehouse. Our store-keepers unpack the cages of stock and help to re-stock the shelves.

▶ A store-keeper and one of the cages of stock.

◀ A sales assistant unpacks a new chest in the gift department.

▲ The manager of the audio and TV department holds the weekly meeting with all his staff.

Department meetings

The managers of all the departments have a five-minute meeting with their staff every day, but on Wednesdays there is always a half-hour meeting before the shop opens. The managers discuss a range of things, such as how well sales are doing, new display stands, labelling the goods or a visit to the department by a manufacturer.

Every morning before the shop opens I spend 45 minutes walking around the store. I make sure all the cages of stock have been unpacked and are off the shop floor. Then I go to a brief staff meeting to check that all the departments have the correct number of staff for the day.

On the shop floor

A manager is in overall charge of each department, but to spread the work and to give responsibility to other members of staff, each department is divided into sections, with their own managers. The sales assistants go to their section manager if they have any problems or questions.

Sales assistants

The job of the sales assistants varies enormously depending on which department they work in. In the soft furnishings department where we sell fabrics, cushions and window-blinds, the sales assistants have to spend more time with customers than, for example, the sales assistants in the stationery department do. All the sales assistants serve customers, make sure the stock is labelled clearly and change the displays.

> I love the variety in my job. Today some customers needed advice about their choice of curtain material, another customer wanted to re-cover his garden chairs and one wanted some material for a wigwam!
>
> Nigel, sales assistant
> Soft Furnishings

◀ A section manager and a sales assistant from the soft furnishings department hang up a range of light, summer curtains. They think about how to display the range of colours so that they look their best.

◀ A section manager and a sales assistant from our linens department change the pillowcases and duvet covers on one of our bed displays. Everything has to be colour co-ordinated.

▼ I talk to the manager of the toy department about some garden toys that have just arrived. I suggest some ways they could be displayed.

New displays

Most departments regularly change their displays because they want to show customers new stock or highlight a new range.

Talking to people

If I have any suggestions on changing a display or if I am unhappy with the way something looks, then I talk to the department manager. Our company has strict guidelines on how every piece of stock should be priced and we like to group together colours and similar things. The customers have to be able to find what they want quickly and they should know right away how much they are.

The display teams

There are seventeen windows on three sides of this store and we change the windows every three weeks. We also change the clothes on the fashion models and other displays inside the shop regularly. We have two teams of six people – one team works on the window displays and the other on displays inside the shop. The person in charge is the Display Manager.

Fashion models

Every morning staff from the 'internal' display team change about twelve fashion models in the shop. Their section manager keeps a rota of everything that needs to be done. Some of the dressers in the team have done display courses at college and others got their jobs because they have a good eye for colour and design.

Changing models
- Each fashion model costs about £650. They are made from fibreglass and can easily break.
- Each wig costs about £70.
- The dressers wear white gloves because grease and dirt on their fingers mark the models.
- Each fashion model has a change of clothes every two weeks.

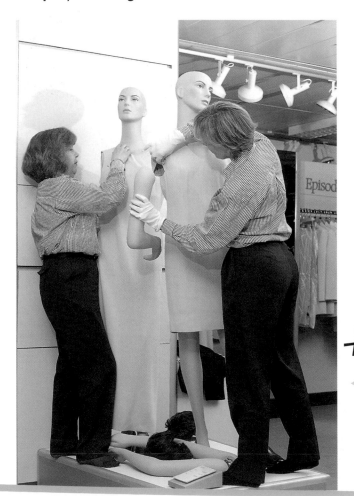

◀ Two dressers change the clothes, wigs and shoes on the fashion models. The arms and legs are easy to remove and slot back in place.

Making the display units

We have a workshop where our carpenter and an assistant make all the display units and panels we need. Staff from the display teams go to the workshop whenever they have to do messy things like covering panels with fabrics. If they need to make up some curtains, we have workrooms at the store too.

People think that we do pretty things all day, but if they saw the amount of covering, moving, lugging and painting we do, they would realise it's not glamorous!

Jo, section manager
Internal Display

▲ One of the dressers from the window display team ties some bamboo together. This will form part of a new display with a Japanese theme.

◀ The carpenter smooths downs a new display unit he is making.

Food and cooking

We have a very busy catering department which has to prepare and cook all the food for staff and customers. The customer restaurant seats about 200 people and opens at 10 o'clock in the morning. We have staff restaurants at the store and in our local warehouses.

Serving customers

We have six different counters in the customer restaurant, serving everything from crepes (pancakes) to home-made soups. There are leaders in charge of each counter who train and manage their staff.

▼ *Staff in the kitchen come in at 8am to start preparing food. We cook a variety of hot meals, cakes and scones every day.*

▲ The Catering section manager talks to the staff on the creperie bar to make sure they have enough toppings and fillings.

▼ Fresh food comes in every day. Carmen has been making salads for us for just over ten years.

Hygiene

Everyone who wants to work in the kitchens and restaurants must pass a test to gain their hygiene certificate. There are very strict rules on handling, cooking and storing food. Any place that serves food is regularly inspected by a government organisation. Our storeman checks that all the food that arrives is properly packed. Then he date-stamps it and makes sure that all the food is stored at the right temperature.

The management meeting

Time for a break. Everyone has a coffee break in the morning and afternoon. The section managers organise rotas for coffee breaks and lunch.

Visit by a buyer

A buyer is someone who is responsible for buying the things we sell. We have a team of buyers based in London for all our stores throughout the country. Buyers need to travel. The fashion buyers, for instance, visit fashion shows, clothes manufacturers and designers all over the world. They have to predict what will be next year's fashions and they have to decide how much to buy – 100, 1000 or 20,000. If the buyers predict the bestsellers, our sales go well and the fashion departments make good profits, but if they make the wrong decisions, our sales suffer and our profits go down.

A weekly update

At midday I go along to our weekly senior managers' meeting. In a busy

◀ *The display manager, deputy services manager, department manager of electrical goods and the staff trainer meet during their coffee break.*

◁ *The menswear buying team models a new range of suits at a sales conference.*

store with nearly 1000 members of staff, it is an ideal opportunity for us all to report on what has been happening in our areas, such as new people starting, the arrival of an important new range and how it will be promoted, any health or safety issues, and the new staff-training courses.

My key responsibilities are to ensure that our profits grow each year and to keep all the staff at the store happy. We want to give everyone here the opportunity to achieve what they want. There are all sorts of careers in this store, all under one roof.

Roger Simmonds, Managing Director

◁ *The Managing Director of the store holds the weekly senior managers' meeting in his office. A new colour sample book has arrived and I am keen to get feedback on some ideas.*

To and from the warehouse

We get all sorts of problems when we're delivering to the customers' homes – roadworks, traffic jams, beds that won't go up a narrow staircase, or dining room units that are too tall to go through the door. Two months ago, we had to remove a bedroom window and then take a new bed up a ladder and in through the window.

Otto, delivery driver

▼ At our local warehouse we keep stock that is ready for collection.

When a customer buys a big item like a sofa or a bed, it has to be delivered to the customer's home. All our deliveries are free. When we make a sale in our furniture department, the computerised till sends the order through to our central warehouse. The warehouse sends stock out to branches of our store throughout the

▲ The shuttle driver makes about 12 journeys a day back and forth between the store and the customer collection warehouse.

Deliveries and collections

- A delivery from our warehouse to a customer's home costs the company on average £5.
- There are on average 500 customer collections a week. This figure goes up to 1500 during the Christmas period.
- In our main local warehouse we stock about 8000 items.
- The delivery drivers make 700 dellveries each week, and double that at Christmas.

country. The stock arrives at our local warehouse at 6am the next day. We have 24 drivers who work in pairs delivering the stock to our customers.

Customer collections

Sometimes customers don't want to carry the things they have bought around town; they would rather pick them up later. We have two minibuses that take their purchases to our collection warehouse – just a few minutes' drive away. Some things like televisions and microwave ovens are stored at this warehouse because we don't have enough space to keep them here.

▼ We have small stockrooms for each department on the shop floor.

Looking after the building and services

When you walk into a department store, it is well lit, the escalators and lifts are running, the temperature is just right and the air-conditioning is on. The services department is responsible for all these things. The department's worst fear is the possibility of a fire breaking out or a power cut. Members of the service team carry out regular checks on all the equipment – fire alarms are tested every day, the engineers check the generators that supply the electricity and the ventilation systems that provide the heat and air-conditioning, and the electricians check the power supplies and the lights.

Shop refits

Sometimes departments move to a new area of the store or they need to expand or change their display area. If the work involves lifting up carpets, pulling up leads and cables, and pulling down shelves and building new ones, then we do this work when the shop is closed. By the time the store re-opens, everything will be back in place, ready for business as usual.

▼ *We keep glass-shelving in stock for new displays.*

I've been here for over 24 years. I know the building backwards. I have to be able to think on my feet. We could have a fire alarm at any minute, overflowing toilets or a major power cut.

Paul, *deputy services manager*

▲ The deputy services manager and a heating and ventilation engineer examine a split air-conditioning pipe.

The boiler room

Our main boilers provide all the hot water and heating for the store. We soften the water here too because hard water makes the dishwashers furr up and the catering department needs to run their dishwashers all day. We have standby water pumps in case of problems with the water supply and we also have a standby electricity generator in case of power cuts.

Facts and figures

- We use about 60,000 litres of water a day in this store. An average household probably uses 50 litres of water a day.
- The department spends £1,500,000 a year.
- One person is employed to change lightbulbs throughout the store and in the lifts. He changes 20,000 bulbs a year!
- Carpenters are known as 'chippies' and electricians as 'sparks'.

Training

Most staff probably do two or three training courses a year. The staff trainer and her three assistant trainers draw up training plans for every employee. They talk to the department managers to assess what training the staff need. There is a wide range of courses, from training on the tills for new recruits to outward-bound courses for management trainees to improve their team-building skills.

Security

Part of everyone's training is to think about how to reduce the amount of stock we waste. Stock can get damaged, broken or lost, and some is stolen. We have store detectives who walk around the shop to look out for any suspicious behaviour from customers. Other members in the security team watch customers on our in-store cameras.

◀ *Management trainees learn to trust each other on this outward-bound course.*

▶ *An assistant staff trainer runs a course in till-training for new recruits. One of the new recruits practises how to key in a sale on a till.*

A member of the security department concentrates as he watches customers on the security cameras.

I started working here in 1983 at Christmas. I found that I enjoyed 'retail' and so I did a three-year course in marketing at night-school and worked here during the day. I set up the electronics and TV department and ran it for two years. I then managed the kitchenware department, which was a complete contrast to electronics. I needed to widen my understanding of the business.

I enjoy working on audio and TV. I like the products. They're always changing and so I can always learn more.

Adrian, department manager
Audio and TV

Serving customers

When new employees arrive, they have to be trained in how to serve customers, how to use the tills and how to organise stock. Experienced staff have developed their skills through knowledge of the departments. The challenge for all department managers is to look at last year's sales figures and beat them. The managers need to look at ways of improving their service to customers through regular training of all their staff. They also try to constantly improve the way they display stock, deal with problems and complaints, and reduce waste.

An experienced sales assistant can give advice to customers. Experience and training helps to improve sales.

Cashing-up

At about 3.30pm the department managers ask their staff to start 'recovery', which means they must start tidying up their departments. At this stage of the day, the shop can look a bit messy. Customers have moved things around, shelves are untidy and clothes in the changing rooms need to go back on the rails.

Emptying the tills

Shortly before we close, the managers and their staff take out the money from the till, put it into bags and separate the cheques and visa payments. They

▲ The manager of the 'trend' fashion department tidies the clothes on the rails.

▶ Cashing-up at the end of the day. Staff can only do this when the last customers have made their purchases.

send the money and the till roll showing all the sales made that day to the accounts department. Staff in accounts check that the amount of money on the till roll matches the money they have received.

Putting away the stock

When the sales assistants tidy items of stock they make sure they 'group' the stock. 'Grouping' means keeping the same or similar items together, so that cups, for example, aren't mixed up with plates and saucers. We try to keep things together so that customers have no trouble finding what they want. We also 'block' items according to colour. 'Blocking' colours means that we keep items of the same colour together.

▼ A sales assistant in the china and glass department tidies the stock at the end of the day.

The shop closes

Late in the afternoon I do my final walk around the store to check that all the stock is back in the right place so that we are ready for the next day. It's also an ideal opportunity for me to give advice to any of the departments.

Security

The security team checks that all the customers have left the store before all the doors are locked. They also make sure that all the alarms have been set.

A new day

Tomorrow morning our buyer for soft furnishings is coming to talk about the new colour scheme for the autumn range of cushions and rugs. It's

▲ I talk to a section manager about the display of clocks and the pricing tickets. All tickets have to be in a neat line, which is our company policy.

▲ All doors are locked and checked by the security team at the end of the day.

Our buyer for soft furnishings shows the department staff the new autumn colour scheme.

The shop has to be thoroughly cleaned before we can open the next day.

important that everyone in the department knows about new ranges so that they can pass on the information to the customers. Our department managers go to sales conferences twice a year where all the new product ranges are highlighted. They bring back the information and pass it on to the rest of their team.

On some days we can have as many as 22,000 sales going through the tills. It can be extremely hectic, but great fun!

Glossary

air-conditioning a process for controlling the temperature and the amount of water in the air; a store with air-conditioning is cooler

buyer a person who buys items the store sells; usually each department has its own buyer

company policy company rules

display units stands on which different products are displayed

dresser a person who arranges displays

employee a person who works for a company

hard water water with a lot of calcium in it, which causes limescale to form

internal display team people who are responsible for the displays inside the shop, including dressing the fashion models

manufacturer a person or business which makes things that will be sold

marketing the business of selling things, including advertising and publicity

outward-bound course adventure training for people: courses aim to improve the way people work together

power cut a loss of electrical power, which affects lighting and heating

profit the money left over after all expenses have been paid

retail selling

rota a list of names showing the order in which people take turns to perform tasks

sales conference a large meeting of buyers and department managers to introduce new ranges of stock and give information on sales

stock the items that are stored and are waiting to be sold in the store

stockroom a room in which items of stock are kept: usually each department has its own stockroom

Index